D1524559

HOT CARS

POSTER BOOK
Mean Machines, Muscle Cars, and Hot Rods

by Jeff Putnam

*Special thanks to
Mark D. Garrett of Garrett Premier Automotive Detailing,
Columbus, Ohio*

Willowisp
Press®

PRINTED IN U.S.A.

Calling all car fans! This Willowisp poster book can be your ticket to dreamland. From vintage American hot rods and growling muscle cars to the absolute latest from legendary European automakers—Ferrari, Lamborghini, Porsche, to name just a few—this book's got them all! So climb into one of these fantastic machines, slip into gear, and step on the accelerator. You're ready for some major excitement!

Hot Car Lingo

autobahn the German name for high-speed freeway or motorway. On many autobahns, there are no speed limits.

air scoop a custom add-on that sucks extra air into high-powered performance carburetors.

customized changed from original condition.

GT Racing a sports car racing circuit for modified street sports cars. (GT stands for Grand Touring).

muscle car an American, mid-'60s car with a very powerful engine. Muscle cars were usually two-door models.

roadster a small, usually two-seated sports car; often a convertible.

Trans Am Racing a road-racing series in which manufacturers compete.

Cover photos by Ron Kimball

Back cover photos by Ron Kimball

Published by Willowisp Press, Inc.
10100 SBF Drive, Pinellas Park, Florida 34666

Printed in the United States of America

2 4 6 8 10 9 7 5 3 1

ISBN 0-87406-634-4

ACURA NSX

First, Japanese auto-builders decided to try the cheap compact car market. Then, they started to build upscale luxury sedans such as the Lexus and Infiniti. Now a Japanese company has taken dead aim at the roughest, toughest market of them all—the high-priced European sports car market dominated by names like Porsche, Ferrari, and Lamborghini. The Acura NSX is like nothing else to come out of the Land of the Rising Sun. Based on Honda's success on the GT Racing circuit and using the company's legendary mechanical and technical pizzazz, this sleek roadster looks ready to take the world by storm.

Photo by Ron Kimball

FERRARI TESTAROSSA

Warning: It's not going to be easy to hop into your family's sedan after looking at this sleek machine. It's one of the world's ultimate fantasy cars, the Ferrari Testarossa. The name means "redhead" in Italian, but it's plain to see that this baby's temperament has nothing to do with color! The Testarossa's top speed is more than 180 miles per hour, and to move that fast you'll have to fork over about a hundred grand! Oh well, you can always *pretend* your family's driving around in the Ferrari.

PORSCHE 959

When you slip behind the wheel of *this* one, you'll definitely feel like you've been struck by lightning! The Porsche has been making sports car fans drool for years. And the new 959 isn't going to change things. The hottest thing from Germany, this nasty Porsche checks in with a top speed of around 180. But it handles like a dream, even when you're cruising down Germany's high-speed *autobahn*. Of course, you might prefer to creep down Main Street in second gear. Why? Because who can see how incredibly sharp your Porsche is at 130 miles per hour?

Photo by Ron Kimball

CHEVROLET CORVETTE

Here it is—America's first production sports car! It was the stuff of dreams when it burst on the scene, and quickly became popular as a great car to cruise around in. In fact, the two-toned jobs, like this ultra-cool '56, are still huge favorites with today's sports car fanatics. Of course, that doesn't mean everyone would trade one of the '50s beauts for today's latest model, which sports a high-tech drive train and space-age electronics.

FORD CUSTOM COUPE

We're talking classic here! It's a 1933 Ford, customized and—judging by those flames—absolutely on fire! This hot rod may be vintage, but when you check out all the components, it's as up to date as you can get. Take a look at those whopper tires on the back, the gleaming chrome air scoop, and that great little rearview mirror on the driver's side window. Makes it easy to keep an eye on what's trailing you!

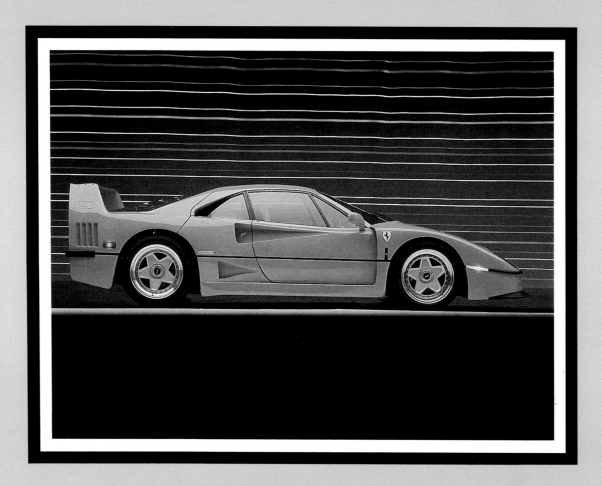

FERRARI F-40

Ready for too-cruel question Number One? You've just won a contest to receive the Ferrari of your choice—absolutely free! All you have to do is choose which one you want. Will it be the black Testarossa Convertible or this incredible, 200 mile-per-hour, 478-horsepower F-40? Easy question, huh? Hint: Both Italian-made beauties will blow your mind *and* knock your socks off, so maybe you'd be better off just choosing by color!

LAMBORGHINI DIABLO

There's no doubt about *this* dream machine! It's the very latest from legendary Italian car builder Lamborghini. The *Diablo* is most definitely a red devil. To get together the money to buy this Lambo, you'd probably have to collect the family cars of every kid in your class and sell them all. But it would be worth it, wouldn't it?

Photo by Ron Kimball

PONTIAC GTO

Once upon a time, when you could practically fuel a car with pocket change, this humongous metal monster ruled the roads. Popularly called the "Goat," the Pontiac GTO was king of the mid-'60s American muscle cars, and it was *the* car to be seen in. Just say the letters and you get a feeling of awesome Detroit born-and-bred power under the hood—tons of chrome, and that low rumble of mega-horsepower from the tailpipe. Like the animal the GTO was nicknamed after, this 1964 had quite a kick.

PORSCHE 928-S

Nobody would disagree that Porsche has produced as many supercars as any other company. But if you want to see people disagree, ask them which is the best Porsche of all time—now, that's major disagreement! A strong candidate, though, is the 928S. As far as a lot of people are concerned, the German-made car is tops in driving perfection, with its silky smooth handling and 316 horses under the hood.

CHEVROLET CAMARO

This muscle car had all the horses it needed to do some major mangling. The Camaro was Chevy's answer to the Ford Mustang, and when it rolled off Chevrolet's production line, it came off with a top-notch set of wheels. In fact, the American-made Camaro beat the Mustang in the Trans Am races the year this one came out. This 1969 model was the hottest of all—the Z 28. Of course, you had to supply your own customized air scoop!

Photo by John Farquhar

FORD MUSTANG GT350

In 1964, a fellow at Ford had an idea: Build an affordable, sporty little car, make sure it's fun to drive, and maybe we can sell a few. That car became a legend and yes, Ford sold a few—million! Coupe, fastback, or the incredibly popular convertible, the Mustang won the hearts of American drivers like no other car before. As with the T-Bird, later Mustangs became big clumsy cars. But the mid-'60s models, like this '65 GT350, were the perfect design for the times. Oh ... and the guy with the idea? He did all right, too. His name's Lee Iacocca, and he rose through the ranks to lead Chrysler with a style as well-known as the Mustang itself.

Photo by Ron Kimball

FORD THUNDERBIRD

Probably one of the most desirable classic cars of them all, the '57 T-Bird is the ultimate dream machine for a lot of people. Just hop in, start the engine, and take off for places unknown. No matter where you're going, this T-Bird will get you there in unmatchable style. Although the T-Bird in later years became a big fat luxury car, the early two-seaters were sporty to the max. Now they're rare and expensive to the max, too!

MERCEDES-BENZ 300SL GULLWING

You'd better believe that this one made some waves back in 1955! Those wild doors made the lucky owner feel like he was climbing into a jet fighter, ready for take-off. Benzes may have a reputation for being well-behaved, ultra-posh limousines. But that famous German engineering and style also went into hot numbers like the Gullwing.

JAGUAR XKE 3.8

Have you ever heard the '60s song "Dead Man's Curve" by Jan and Dean? In it, a spanking new Jag XKE can't handle a nasty bend in the road and ends up at the bottom of a cliff. Well, that might have been the only curve this lean and mean machine couldn't handle. You can bet this British beauty turned lots of heads with its sleek lines, awesome power plant, and leather-covered interior. The XKE 3.8 was a classic combination of English elegance and racing car spunk, and if you want to buy one today, it'll only cost you a small fortune!

Photo by Ron Kimball

1952 MG, 1954 AUSTIN HEALEY, 1962 MGA 1600

Take a good look at this trio of classic convertibles. The setting may be stately, but ask anyone to list the all-time most fun cars and chances are you'll get an earful about these nifty little English sports cars. You can be sure that the spunky MG, Austin-Healey, and Triumph will live forever. After all, they *are* the grandparents of today's mean machines from Italy, Germany, and the U.S.! Besides, is there anything to match the sensation of cruising down a country lane, shifting gears, and feeling the wind on your skin as you grip that polished walnut steering wheel?

Photo by Ron Kimball